TEA-SPIRATION

Inspirational Words for Tea Lovers ♥

Lu Ann Pannunzio
from theteacupoflife.com

happy steeping & sipping

For my fellow tea lovers, especially my sister, Luciana, who gave me my very first cup of tea and ignited my passion for the beverage.

"Forget what you've been told about tea, all those dos and don'ts. **Tea-spiration** takes the practice of appreciating tea back to basics. Lu Ann offers practical tips on how to get the most out of a cup of tea, and shows us how any tea drinker is already a tea expert."

- Bonnie Eng, Thirsty for Tea blog

"A thoughtful and refreshing look at how we should think of tea, prepare it, drink it, and allow it to change our lives. It is a helpful, down-to-earth guide for anyone who has never really stopped to think about the significance of tea, about the enjoyment to be had from every single cup, and about the benefits that tea can bring to everyday life."

- Jane Pettigrew, Tea Historian and Tea Educator

"Where will your next cup of tea take you? A trip down memory lane? Or, swept away to another region of the world? When was the last time you truly experienced something through all five senses? The heart of this book is that of a tea lover. Allow yourself to experience tea as described within and you just may find **Tea-spiration** to live a more meaningful life thanks to this healthful, delicious beverage (tea) and our affini-tea for it."

- Gail Gastelu, Owner/Publisher,
The Tea House Times

"Reading **Tea-spiration** brought me the same feeling as sipping a fresh cup of tea, soothing and mind-opening. The non-judgmental notion Lu Ann poured into her writing is the true offering of tea that is often overlooked in our busy everyday life."

- Li Gong, Ph.D., Founder of
Encha Organic Matcha

"In **Tea-spiration** it is evident that Lu Ann Pannunzio approaches the topic of tea drinking as a state of meditation; a mindful practice that encourages leaving behind hectic daily living.

Without technical information on the makings of tea, it will make a great gift for any tea lover as well as inspire novice tea drinkers to sit down with a cup of tea. This book reminds me of the poem by Hamamoto Soshun: "Chanoyu should be made with the heart, not with the hand. Make it without making it, in the stillness of your mind".

As a practicing yogi I see the parallels in tea drinking and the yogic path. I look forward to having a copy of my own to support me as I refresh my mind and hydrate my body during contemplative moments in my daily living.

Namaste"

- **Emily Slonina**, author of Anywhere Anytime Any Body Yoga, using yoga in everyday life.

"Lu Ann Pannunzio's **Tea-spiration** is a beautifully written book that reminds us all to be present and mindful of every steeped moment. She lets us in on her tea rituals and memories, while encouraging us to have the freedom to take a step back and shape our own tea experiences. Her kind and knowledgeable tone of voice makes you feel as though you are a friend chatting with her over a cup of tea in her kitchen. This is a must-read for tea beginners to experienced sippers, as it grounds one in the meditative and sensory ritual of tea. Lu Ann gently guides you to craft personal steeping rituals and discover tea's deeper meaning in your own life."

- **Alexis Siemons,** Tea Consultant and Writer, Teaspoons & Petals

Table of Contents

FOREWORD

When Margit and I planted *Camellia sinensis* on our farm in 2010 we did not know where the experiment would take us on our tea journey. Six years later on July 1st we served Canada's first single origin estate grown organic tea. Folks from near and far have since come to our tea room to taste the terroir of locally grown tea served in Margit's handbuilt ceramic teaware. We have also shipped our rare tea to collectors and tea lovers across Canada and the World.

Our humble little idea has attracted a lot of attention over the years and we have had interest from newspapers and television, various other media including bloggers, guide books, lifestyle magazines and more. We have shared our story many times in many ways and there is one individual who has truly stood out as having best captured our journey to craft Canada's finest tea and redefine the Canadian approach to tea culture and artisanal tea creation and that person is Lu Ann Pannunzio.

Her approach to writing about us was like the preparation of a fine cup of tea. She took the time to build a relationship around sincere curiosity, authenticity and an appreciation and respect for the tea. It was simple and easy to share our successes and failures with our tea growing experiment and our adventure to create the most authentic tea and clay experience we possibly can.

As a result of our exchange Lu Ann wrote an article for Fresh Cup, a leading tea and coffee industry magazine distributed across North America. Her in depth reportage and resonant approach turned our story into the feature article and magazine cover. Released at the World Tea Expo in Las Vegas, our Canadian tea journey was shared far and wide because of Lu Ann's dedication and artfulness to write about something very close to her heart.

It is my priviledge to be part of her endeavour to write this insightful and inspiring book. Whether you are new to tea or if you are a tea expert, Lu Ann will ease you back into what is important and meaningful in the simple beauty of a cup of tea. She is gracious enough to not assume to be your guide but rather creates an environment in which you become the master of your own tea ritual.

I often stand amongst the tea plants in the early morning mist holding my favourite Margit clay mug and smile knowing that when the farm gates open the world invites itself in to share our Canadian tea culture experience. Tea-spiration will take you on your most authentic tea journey and will grow your love of tea as you fill your cup of life.

Read. Sip. Enjoy.

Victor Vesely

Tea Maker

Westholme Tea Farm

Vancouver Island, BC Canada

INTRODUCTION

(WHY THIS BOOK EXISTS)

Tea-spi-ra-tion

noun

*- being inspired to do, create or feel something
extraordinary, all thanks to tea.*

One of the things I love about the paths
through life is the focus on appreciating the
simple things. Like when you get the chance to
pop fresh bubble wrap, sleep in freshly-washed
bed sheets or even eat that last slice of cake
before someone else gets to it. All of these satisfying little moments can lead to a great big life.
What is my most favorite simple thing in life?
Tea. Some might argue that tea isn't very simple,
but if you see it that way then it can be.

When you think of tea, what is the first thing
that comes to mind? Give yourself some time
to consider exactly what tea means to you. Jot
it down physically or mentally. Got it? Great! If
you are thinking of something along the lines of
soothing, inspiring, or even meditative, then you
are on the right track. Tea has many beautiful
qualities, versatility being a big one. But, sometimes, we can find ourselves getting so caught

up in what "tea" we can use next to detox or lose weight that we forget the true meaning of tea. Yes, tea does have its benefits, but when we focus too much on those, the point of tea is misconstrued. Let these thoughts go and make more space for those that truly count.

Tea is similar to life in the sense that you need to pay closer attention to the little things, as they make for the happiest journey. You will lose a lot of those little things if you live your life just looking forward to the big moments. If you begin to see tea as something more than just dried leaves in water, then you will find it more enjoyable, and there is a chance you will learn more about yourself along the way.

I have been learning from the leaf itself since I started my blog, where I always write with a cup of tea by my side. The most common question I receive is: "Why do I love tea so much?" It is my home, my ritual, my relief, and my meditation. My daily tea rituals keep me grounded. They make me feel great inside and out. My blog is called The Cup of Life because tea is just that.

Don't let anyone fool you – tea is for everyone. With thousands of tea varieties available, there is bound to be at least one tea that is meant for you. For me, it all started with a strawberry flavored black tea bag. A strawberry flavored tea bag that I didn't really think about prior to steeping. I just knew it was something I had to try and hopefully like. With the simple act of boiling water in a kettle, I was presented with a delightful beverage that changed my world. I began the ritual of tea at a young age, and I am grateful that it has continued on my journey of life that I get to share. I am passionate not only about helping people find more than one way to enjoy the beverage, but also reminding them of the art and beauty that comes with tea. I believe one can take the simple act of sipping and use it to change their life for the better. I know tea has the ability to make me happy, calm and just feel good overall. My intention behind this book is to show others how they can feel this way, too.

Tea-spiration is not a textbook-style read where you learn about the history of tea, types of tea or proper steeping instructions. There are plenty of great tea books like that already available. I believe it is time for a book that touches on the little moments with tea that are easily missed and underappreciated. This book exists to change the way people see, think and drink tea. It is where we will dive deeper into the stimulating qualities of tea that are more than just an encouraging quote attached to the tag on your tea bag. I hope that if your answer to the opening question was anything other than something describing the taste or feeling of tea that you will learn more about what it can offer in the end.

That being said, there is no right or wrong way to make tea. To begin to properly enjoy tea, you have to prepare it the way you would like it. It's your cup and no one else's. Go ahead and pour that milk in, add a sweetener, or drink it straight. We won't even argue that you should be drinking loose leaf or tea bags because that's really not the point here. There will be no judgments in these pages. Creating something that is your own is part of the fun and experience.

See all of your tea essentials along with the quality, the shape and color of the dry tea leaves and liquor.

 Smell the perfume and aromas releasing around you from the dry tea leaves and liquor in your cup.

 Hear the sounds of the water and tea being poured into the kettle and cups.

 Feel the texture of your cup through each sip, any refreshing steam and emotions the tea provides.

 Taste an array of flavors, all that the end product has to present.

Just remember to stop and take the time to appreciate what you are drinking.

While reading this book, I encourage you to steep yourself a cup of tea and be prepared to complete all acts throughout the process mindfully. This will allow you to fully appreciate the words you are absorbing and will give you the best tea experience yet. If we make tea too logical, then the happiness it provides can diminish, and you may miss the full, genuine experience.

Get your senses ready too. You will soon notice that all five are used in unique ways for tea drinking.

Why don't you put the kettle on, pick out your favorite cup and tea, and flip the page. Let's get steeping, sipping and reading…

PART I

Starting With An Empty Cup

The beginning. It just might be the most un-
derrated and overlooked step. How does your
tea ritual start? How you begin can ultimately
decide how you will continue throughout.
Different situations can affect how you embark
on your tea session. Perhaps you just woke up
and need to get your tea ready quickly to head
out the door for work. Maybe you just can't
wait to wrap your hands around the warm cup
any longer, or you are finally getting the time
to sit back and relax after a long day. This step
is where it all begins. Start it off the way you
believe is right for you.

The entire process of preparing tea can be
quite meditative. You can have your tea from a
tea bag or even in instant form. But, I believe

you will find loose-leaf tea is the best invest-
ment to help you experience the messages I'm
sharing throughout these pages. Tea bags or
some instant tea products are not always hor-
rible options. But the joy of tea is experiencing
the entire beauty it has to share. These on-the-
go type products are considered short cuts. You
can still enjoy your tea with them, especially if
that is all you have right now; however, there
may be some moments you miss without
loose leaf.

The Arrival of Your Tea Order

Doorbell rings or doors open. Order confirma-
tion appears or card swipes. Whether you shop
in store, or online, purchasing something new
can be thrilling. Take yourself back to how your
tea order arrived. The feelings of answering

the front door to a package or arriving home with a bag in hand are exciting, especially if you have been eyeing an item in-store for a while or stalking the tracker for your online splurge. Something that is new and unique is bound to catch your eye, whether you are aware of it or not. This goes for anything, of course. But for tea products, when you know, you know. There are tea wares available with an elegant design, fresh batches of tea leaves just waiting to be homed, or a tasty sounding tea blend that needs us to test it. Either way, your tea journey begins with that doorbell or that walk through the door.

Creating Your Sanctuary

The one reoccurring theme that you will find in these pages is that tea should slow you down. It is not meant to be a quick, to-go and pick-me-up beverage constantly. There are going to be times when you can't rush the steeping process, and you can't rush your pleasure. Instead, especially here, sitting with your tea is recommended.

Find yourself a clear physical space where you feel most comfortable and have little distraction. Indoors or outdoors, look around and claim your personal area. It may be an empty corner, a spot by the window with the best scenery, or even under a tree with the perfect amount of shade. This is *your* tea space. *Your* tea sanctuary. Make it *your* own. Add extraordinary pictures, tea quotes, books, trinkets, pillows or light music.

The way I see it, I'm more inclined to actually drink my tea and take time doing so when I have a space devoted to my tea time. A tea space kind of reminds me of a cooking space.

Do you ever find it difficult to get the motivation to cook in a kitchen that may feel crowded, not done up to your liking or even just not there? Something like that makes me just want to go out for food or order in, even if I already have all the ingredients for a particular dish. I need a space for just tea in the moment so I don't ever get the feeling that I should just run out to the nearest café for the convenience, even if I already have all the tea I want at home. We need a space to make it feel like our own and make us want to actually be present with our tea. Do anything you need to do that will make you love your tea space, feel an exceptional vibe, and want to be there often to make it a routine. As long as you have the chance for quiet and peaceful moments with tea, it can be wherever and however you would like. For as long as you are in this tea space created by you, you are home.

Choosing The Right Tea Ware for the Right Tea

In various cultures, the tea ware you actually decide to use for your tea time is an important aspect to beginning. Many not only grow their own tea, but also construct their own tea ware to use during their tea ceremonies. It is common to have specific vessels devoted just to tea and the more attractive you find your tea vessel to be, the more inclined you are to use it and perhaps make tea a daily ritual. Choose a shape that forms well in your hands and colors that bring you happiness to help you relax. However, keep in mind that when settling on a vessel for your tea, it should not be done forcefully. To do so mindfully, select the tea ware you feel the most drawn to at the moment or the one you think will best suit the tea it will hold shortly.

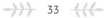

Look through your endless collection of tea-pots and teacups or mugs. Like the leaf itself, some tea wares have their own stories to share. In order to truly be able to appreciate your tea ware, you need to understand at least some history behind it. Your tea ware could be a mug you received as a gift from an event you attended, a vintage teacup passed down to you, or even made by hand from clay. There is value to all. This is your time to hold your teapot or cup and put yourself in the shoes of the person who gifted it to you or, taking it a step deeper, the person who constructed it. Take a closer look at the characteristics of each. Notice any rustic forms, [how the texture feels in your hands] beautifully engraved embellishments, and even any imperfections. What may not seem perfect to you could have easily been seen as perfection in the creator's eyes.

Sitting on my shelf is a teapot that I adore, more so for what lies behind it. It is large and round in shape, ceramic and glazed with several drips captured along the sides. The spout is short, and sometimes I stare at it wondering how it became that way, not proportioned to its body. The handle is made of tough, straw-like pieces that are braided together and always standing upright, something I always felt was the wrong decision for such a heavy build. All of these thoughts run through my mind as I admire the hand-built piece, telling me that it should be changed to make it completely perfect. But lately, I have been learning to embrace and welcome the beauty in the naturally imperfect world. This follows an ancient Japanese philosophy known as *Wabi Sabi*. *Wabi Sabi* celebrates beauty in what is natural, flaws and all. Just by holding a piece of hand-built tea ware, you can feel the difference in its nature from something that has been mass-produced. If you learn to welcome the handmade and irregularly shaped tea ware and abandon "perfection" during your tea time, then you can begin to see the stories of those who provided the vessels for you. You can create your own thoughts on the matter to make it uniquely yours. This is not limited to handmade items. The same can be said for your cracked souvenir mug or the sentimental teacup from grandma.

No matter what you have, it is important to appreciate the work that went into your tea ware and, later, to celebrate by filling it with your most enjoyable tea. Beginning with this empty cup is your first step to truly enjoying and giving yourself completely to tea. But what does giving yourself to tea actually mean? It means letting go. It means building trust. It means focusing on what matters. It means taking the time to see what is right in front of you and allowing yourself to relax and see what is in store.

Selecting the Perfect Tea that was Picked Just for You

There is a tea appropriate for any time, any circumstance and any situation. When it comes time to pick out your tea of choice, it can all depend on how you feel in the moment.

With six different types of tea — — —

Black   *Green*   *White*

Yellow   Oolong   Puerh

you can find a cup made just for you. Are you
dreaming of the taste of your favorite tea, need-
ing a pick me up or minute of calm? Perhaps
you are considering trying that tea that you
have saved for a special occasion. Whichever is
the case, you are in control.

When you have your tea and are ready to
scoop the leaves out for the steeping process,
stop yourself. Before you open the packaging
and dig in, take a moment to read about the
tea you just chose, whether you have to search
for information online or it is made available
to you right on the label. Feel and examine the

packet up close— whether it is an airtight tin or resealable pouch—before you find the hidden treasures inside. Ask yourself a few questions here about the tea's journey. Where do these tea leaves come from? What are the conditions there? Who was the tea farmer? When were these tea leaves harvested? The region a tea is grown in and the decisions made by famers and workers affect your tea's flavor, appearance, aroma and other qualities. Think of these tea leaves as your window into their lives and their efforts.

Afterwards, gently open the packaging and take a look at the contents inside. Jot down or make mental notes of some key characteristics that stand out to you. Focus on the quality of the dry leaves along with its colors and shapes. Certain tea leaves are shaped the way they are for a reason. Certain tea leaves are shaded differently in color for a reason.

Begin to imagine more about the harvesting and processing methods that these leaves went through for you.

Next time you sit down with a cup of tea, just stop and envision your tea growing on a plant, being handpicked and then traveling through a lengthy process just to find its way into your

WATER IS LIFE'S CONNECTOR

US

EARTH

TEA

The one major thing we all
have in common is that we are
all made up of water. We need it
to grow and survive.

Water gives us all life.

cup. Learning the deeper roots of where your tea is coming from will bring you closer to the tea and all it has to offer. You may find yourself savoring your leaves a little more than usual.

Drawing Fresh, Pure Water to Make Your Tea

Tea is special because it combines earth, water and fire all in one. However, out of these three components, I would consider water to be the single most important element of tea.

Without water, you simply would not be able to enjoy the beverage that comes next to it as the world's most consumed. Water can easily be something we take for granted, the most no matter how (in) accessible it can be for some. Do you know where your water comes from? Where the water for tea you drink comes from? As it is essentially 99% of what you are drinking, you should care as much about the water you are using as the tea.

To experience the best quality when preparing tea, using freshly drawn water where possible is essential. Describing something in its pure form that is odorless and colorless is challenging, but simplicity is what makes it easy to love. Next time you have fresh water in front of you to fill your kettle, think about where it is coming from and how accessible it is to you. Did you have a tap to flip on, or did you have to walk miles away to collect the water? If you have easy access to water, consider those who may not and the struggles that can follow. Think about just how precious this clean, hydrating beverage is to have available to you whenever you need or want it.

While waiting for the water in the kettle to boil, here is a moment we should take advantage of even if it is a small window of peaceful opportunity. If you think about it, it is the perfect time to erase your thoughts and just focus on the task at hand. The kettle provides a faint whistle to concentrate on before this heated water gives you the liquid wisdom you're waiting for.

Breathe.

The heat provides steam to focus on and trick your mind into staying in the present tea moment.

Breathe.

Water will bring your tea to life. Without it your leaves will never dance with the grace and beauty that one witnesses as they pour this liquid over their dry leaves.

PART II

Opening a Freshly-Sealed Package of Tea

Peel or cut open the seal that is treasuring the contents inside the package. Close your eyes and allow the tea's invigorating aroma to escape for the very first time. Can you identify your tea just from the aroma it gives off?

Whether it is scented or not, there can be many different aromas that come within a single tea. The dry leaves can produce notes that may be slightly or even extremely varied from those they produce when they are steeping or when they are wet and spent. But possibly the most satisfying aroma comes from that instant you finally get around to breaking the seal of a new or old tea purchase. Inhaling the fresh leaves that have been sealed up for some time immediately releases a scent that takes you away for as long as you will let it. Certain scents can trigger specific emotions and memories. This is where more hidden treasures from tea are uncovered. Scents are so closely linked to memory that the feelings your tea will bring will be entirely unique to you. The examples I give will apply to me.

When I smell a tea that is blended or straight with sweet notes of strawberries, it takes me back to the first tea bag that started it all. I can see my younger self sitting at the long, wooden table with my mother and sister at the other end. I can hear the hard, loud whistle from a stovetop kettle, as the water gets hotter and hotter. Light chatter and the clinking of irregular shaped mugs and silver teaspoons fill the air. Sitting at the brown chairs that matched the kitchen tiles and cupboards, I sat with my feet barely touching the ground.

But all that mattered were my lips touching the mug of tea.

Usually when I inhale the grassy fragrance of a Sencha green tea, or other similar Japanese green teas, I am reminded of the times I spent outdoors enjoying the fresh air and watching my dad cut the lawn. Occasionally I am even just brought back to when I would be sitting inside near open windows hearing the sounds of the lawn mower that let me know of his whereabouts. These positive memories are all brought back from just a soft inhale of tea.

Think over this moment for a while right now. Go ahead and open a fresh package of tea or envision yourself doing so. You are the first person to get to experience these tea leaves that were picked, processed and packaged to get to you today.

Inhale.

Depending on the exact freshness of the tea, the aroma has been sealed in from production up until now. Nothing is better than that initial escape.

Taking a few good deep breaths allows you to experience the tea's aroma and gives you time to close your eyes and stay in the present moment. Eliminate negative thoughts, concerns or worries. Unfortunately, most of our time is spent thinking about the past or the future, rather than facing the present moment. The present moment is the only period in which you can experience every characteristic of your tea. I hope you find your tea is full of good aromas, good feelings and good memories.

This Is All For You

There was a time, believe it or not, when I did not love tea as much as I do today. Of course, that could be easy to say because of the simple fact that my love and passion for the beverage continues to grow, but this goes beyond that. In that time. I began to reduce my intake as I found that the pleasure I [would] get from an uplifting cup of tea escaped me altogether. It did not matter if I switched the tea I was drinking or if it was hot or iced. There was something else missing in the tea – me.

I wasn't fully experiencing tea. I had a habit of turning the kettle on and walking away to focus on other things in life until the kettle would whistle, calling for me to return. Sometimes even then it would take me a while longer to come back. I was fixated on other things that I thought deserved more of my attention.

I later came to realize that tea was not the problem, I was. In life, we can get frustrated when others tell us how to do things a certain way. It can be something as little as critiquing

the way you clean your room, or something
even bigger like how to control your financ-
es. Criticism is difficult to handle when it is
mean-spirited, or the subject is dear to our
hearts. This is how I felt after being informed
by others and the media that there was a right
way to make tea, and I was doing it "wrong" all
this time. Not experiencing tea properly and
doing tea wrong are two separate things. Why
was making tea such a gratifying experience if I
was doing it wrong this entire time? To experiment, I followed the "right" ways to make and
drink my tea. That is when I found myself dislik-
ing it little by little. By following others' rules, I
was no longer making *my* tea.

Tea is whatever you would like it to be. Is there
a right way or wrong way to taste tea? The
simple answer is: if it tastes good to you, then
it is right. Don't overthink it – just slow down.

Ignore the countless critics on the proper way to enjoy tea whether from another person or in the media. Every cup has its own story to tell and you do not want to miss that by being so fixated on the rights and wrongs that don't exist. Tea is whatever you would like it to be.

When the First Leaf Begins to Unfurl

One of the most lovable aspects of tea is the visual beauty. Whether you are observing the dry leaves or the liquor, you may become aware of and experience the inner tranquility tea provides. Awareness is not only about seeing what is right in front of you. Consider what you could be ignoring in that moment, and be aware of the mental distractions.

The step between the dry leaves and liquor, steeping, is the best time to fully immerse yourself and pay attention to your surroundings. It may be the most impatient part as we are just waiting for the chance to indulge, but it is also one of the most crucial steps towards preparing tea and creating your gratification.

Short buds, long leaves, hand rolled or even hand tied: all tea leaves provide the perfect opportunity to focus on them dancing in the water, expanding and extracting full flavor, color, and aroma.

I find this step to be one of the most meditative of them all. For some, focusing on one set object makes meditating easier. Here is where you can do just that with your tea:

Calm your mind.

Focus on the tea.

Place the tea leaves in a teapot.

Pour hot water over the tea leaves.

Watch as the tea leaves unfurl for you.

You are literally watching one liquid turn into another. Do not judge what you are observing; this is not the time to analyze. Watch as the water warms up the leaves and creates movements throughout. Picture the tea leaves as a recent problem or situation in your life that is currently unraveling before your eyes and solving itself when the steeping process is complete. Negative situations can make you feel small compared to what you have to face.

However, size has nothing to do with strength. In this case, in just a matter of minutes, something that was small became quite powerful and created something positive. Even the tiniest of objects can produce something magical. What you see while your tea leaves unfurl and dance around in your steeping vessel is meant for you.

The Hands That Touched the Leaves and Brought this Tea to Life

It is a warm morning with the sun pouring down on the ready and luscious green *Camellia sinensis* plants. In the fields canvased by the living beings, tea pickers are plucking each leaf from the plant by hand to be placed in a woven basket and carried off to its next journey. There is a lot more to be said about the tea you are about to enjoy than you may think. It may not seem like much

goes into a little leaf, but the tea plant is one that requires a lot of patience and labor. Many people devote their lives to this amazing plant. Have you ever wondered who is the individual that started the preparation of your tea? Whether they are near or far, the connection you have with them is real thanks to your tea. They hand plucked the leaves that now bring you joy.

Their single touch brought the leaves to life and now you are responsible to bring them more life. We should give many thanks throughout a tea session, but these people are among the most deserving of our gratitude.

Knowing even the slightest bit of information about where the different leaves in your tea stash came from can enhance your tea drinking ritual. One of the easiest ways to get lost in your tea moment is sitting, sipping and thinking of how the tea leaves arrived from the tea farm to your cup right in this moment. Keep in mind that growing tea is a slow process that requires patience. The tea plant, *Camellia sinensis*, should be about three years old before the leaves can be harvested and shared. Imagine how old the plant your tea came from is. Imagine the farmers who wake up every morning to tend to the tea plants. Imagine the workers who pick and process the tea leaves, creating and sharing the stories behind each leaf.

Always remember those who work behind the scenes for your tea. If it were not for them, what would you be drinking in this moment?

Cold Hands, Warm Tea

There is a curious saying: "cold hands, warm

heart." It means that individuals with cold hands are warmer on the inside, with loving and kind personalities. In this case, whether or not your hands are cold, the tea is warm. The tea is warm with love, and now it is being distributed to you.

As you grasp your cup of tea for the first time, your hands touch the soothing warmth before your insides. I used to love a moment like this when I was younger, before my tea days. Whether I woke up cold or came inside from a chilly day, the first thing I wanted was something to warm up my hands. At the time, that something was hot chocolate. My instant reaction was to pour water into the stovetop kettle, turn on the burner and get out the chocolate powder. Looking back at my reaction, I didn't just need heat. I wanted it. That craving affects my tea drinking today.

Do not look at warmth just in terms of tem-

perature here. Yes, the cup of tea is heating up your cold hands perfectly. But what else is it offering? It is a positive welcoming that brings comfort to you both mentally and physically. The warmth that is radiating from the tea is the first notable sign of the energy it contains:

Energy from the earth and soil in which the tea plants lived their lives.

Energy from the water the tea plants drank to stay hydrated.

Energy from the sunlight that the tea plants absorbed for more nutrients.

Energy from the workers who cared for the tea plants.

Holding that warm cup of tea in your cold hands prepares your body and mind for the soothing energies and comfort you will experience within the first few sips.

A Spa Experience in a Cup

Tranquility, serenity, rejuvenation – these are all words that are typically used to describe a spa experience. These terms can also be used to portray your tea session. Similar to a spa treatment, exfoliating steam from your cup is gently covering your face. Close your eyes and enjoy the refreshment while it cleanses and purifies. As the steam that the cup of tea is emitting calms down slowly, open your eyes. Look down at your cup of tea and witness the color. Is it bright? It is pale? Is it green? Is it red?

A cup of tea offers you a short, peaceful pause from the busy routines of your daily life. However, this little moment is particularly helpful if you are feeling under the weather because the steam from a hot cup of tea is reviving. It can be light and refreshing or strong and clearing. The difference depends on the water temperature needed for the type of tea you prepared. Allow the steam to soothe your nerves and wash worries away, to open the door for new opportunities to come like that first sip of the tea.

Part III

Let's Get Sipping

I find that it can take up to three sips to understand your tea. For a positive tasting, I like to experience those three sips with three separate intentions.

First Sip Intention

 I am remaining absolutely open-minded. The first impression will be judgment free.

The First Sip of the Freshly Steeped Tea

Here is the moment you have been waiting for. Whether it was since you first opened your eyes after a rest or since you got in from a busy day, this is what has been on your mind from the start. This is the moment where you get to taste what you just created. This is where you

get to feel the soothing beverage and bask in the awesomeness of the tea. Suddenly everything feels alive, achievable and completely possible. Nothing beats the first sip of a great tea. It makes you really wonder what you have been doing without this beverage before.

Usually when I begin to taste a tea, I have a notepad and pen by my side to jot down any tasting notes so that I can remember and share later on in my writings. My absolute favorite part, included in my tea reviews, is a section called "First Sip Thought." I added this small description because I think it is essential to document how I feel or what I felt when that very first sip of new (to me) tea was taken, as it usually leads to many other great things to say in a review. However, I do not limit this idea to just when I know I am going to be reviewing a tea. It is a reoccurring feeling that I like to think about because sometimes just a couple random words of feelings says it all about a tea.

A first sip thought does not have to be something quite elaborate. It is literally the first thing that comes into your mind during or right after that first sip of tea, whether it be a full sentence of just one word of exclamation. It is also good to remember that these are your tasting notes. Everyone has a distinctive palate. So while you may notice something in a certain tea, another may have noticed something entirely different. And that's okay. To have several means to describe a single sip is just another reason tea is exquisite.

To give you an idea, here are some examples of "First Sip Thought" that I have documented in the past:

For a floral masala chai blend, "a mix of spring and fall"

For a lavender white tea blend, "sweet dreams"

For a roasted oolong with sweet and milky notes, "a creamy, caramelized dessert"

For a green tea with vegetable stock characteristics, "soup season"

You might even compare the first sip feeling to chills that you would get while listening to certain music or viewing various stunning art forms. It is all a similar feeling of bliss or awe in the beauty and flavor of tea when it first hits your palate. Taking the first sip of a tea can release a rush of emotions, especially if the tea is exceedingly good. If you are patient enough, and love what you are drinking, you can feel the same at any stage of the tea session as long as you open yourself to the tea and welcome everything that happens.

Second Sip Intention

 I will reassure myself of the tea's taste and become familiar with it.

Going Back for a Second Sip

Someone once told me that after the first sip, no matter how wonderful it was, the next few sips are where you get to really know the tea. The first sip is where you get to feel the taste. The following are where you are able to know the tea like a friend. Your relationship with tea should be similar to a close friendship. Your first

sip is just like your first impression, and the second and third sips are where you are willingly reconnecting to grow the relationship.

Like a friend, tea can adapt to how you are feeling. If you are feeling down, tea can lift up your spirits. If you are feeling accomplished, tea can help you celebrate. If you are feeling tired, tea can bring you to a relaxed state. There is a tea to fit every emotional reaction that a friendship can.

While indulging in your second sip, feel the warm tea in your mouth and follow it when it travels down. Note how it feels. Are you feeling the same thing you did initially, or has it evolved into something more since the first sip? Is it full-bodied? Light and fresh? Observe the friend-like bond that comes along as the sip passes.

Third Sip Intention

 I will decide how the tea makes me feel and if it is *worthy of my collection.*

The Third Sip and Many More To Come

You took the time to prepare the tea the way you prefer, and now you should take your time and not rush to finish your cup of tea. Unlike other beverages, tea should be appreciated sip by sip not gulp by gulp. This way you can sincerely welcome the distinctive flavors.

> *Tea is slow.*

> *In growing.*

> *In drinking.*

In enjoying.

It makes sense. Good things take time.

By now, the tea should be felt within you. Your relationship with it is continually growing, and here is where you can decide if you will stay with it.

If you disliked the tea, that's okay, too. I hate to say it, but there can be bad tea out there. I'm not just talking about a bad tasting because you may have prepared it in an unusual way. I am strictly talking about the tea itself here. This is where tea and you become more like a relationship. "It's not you, it's me," says tea. However, sometimes, I would beg to differ. If I came across a tea and I didn't care much for the taste, I would not give up on it right away. I would constantly try that same tea over and

over again—different preparation, new mindset—
and if I still just could not get myself to favor it,
then I would reevaluate. "But all the reviews I read
prior to ordering spoke so highly of this tea," I
would think, "It must just be me." Wrong.

Imagine if I thought that way about food?
Coming from an Italian family, the easiest thing
for me to compare it to would be homemade
pasta sauce. Pasta seemed like a considerably
affordable meal for a college student. So when
I moved away from home, it was my first away
meal. However, when you grow up eating pasta
with homemade tomato sauce, you can quickly
become disappointed. Needless to say, I disliked
the pasta. I disliked my once-favorite meal. It
was too sweet. It had no substance. It was
store bought sauce. "But I come from an Italian
background, it must just be me," I thought. I
quickly finished the sauce and never purchased

it again. Just like if I come across a bad tea today, I accepted the fact that it is not for me, finished it off, and did not put it in my cart again.

Reviews for teas, or any other products, are an excellent resource but not something we should solely rely on. They are tremendous for introducing you to a tea, but never bring a review that is not your own into a tea tasting. When savoring your tea sip by sip, you should not think about someone else's thoughts on it or else your tea is no longer personal. If a reviewer liked the tea, it does not guarantee you will or vice versa.

* Do not worry if they say it is mediocre. If you like the tea, you like it.

* Do not worry if they say it is superior. If you dislike the tea, you dislike it.

It is important to note that if you are drinking a tea you do not like, allow yourself to feel that way. Allow yourself to dislike the tea and label it as bad in your books. As you refine your palate, you can always come back to this "bad" tea and give it another chance. For now, move on to the next sip, or the next tea entirely, so you can taste the other delights out there for you.

Hearing What Your Tea Has To Say

Listening is one of the most valuable skills an individual can learn in today's society.

Children learn and grow by listening.

Students learn and grow by listening.

Employees learn and grow by listening.

We all learn and grow by listening.

Listening allows us all to really connect better and be fully present. So what happens if we utilize our listening skills with tea?

I am sure you have heard all the standard rules that deal with tea, but the truth is: tea is personal. No two teas are alike and no two palates are alike. When you are drinking tea, it is basically a private conversation between the tea and your individual soul. If you are drinking a tea that is respectable to you, then it will take you on a secluded journey to your own oasis.

I can sit here and tell you that you need to use three grams of tea leaves for eight ounces of water, or list all the essentials to preparing the most perfect cup, but have you ever just stopped and listened to what your tea may be trying to tell you? Let yourself learn from the leaf. Focus on just the tea leaves here and pay no attention to the tea ware and other diverse tea accessories you may have to use. They won't matter much in terms of creating a delicious beverage. If all you have is water, tea and a bowl or cup, then I would say you are off to the best start of making a pleasant-tasting tea.

Whether you prepared a green tea or a black tea, each tea is going to provide you with something entirely different from the other. After your first three sips, you may have noticed the offerings. This is where you can pay closer attention to what your tea is trying to tell you. With this third sip, bring yourself back to the first and second. Examine how the tea has made you feel the last few sips, and see what it will allow you to change for a new outcome. Listen to how it feels, the flavors and aromas it ignites, the appearance of the leaves and water. Experiment from there.

You will learn more about the tea, and how exactly it wants to be prepared and appreciated, just by listening.

Finding the Perfect Pair for that Cup of Tea

Maybe tea by itself isn't for you. If you find this to be true, then I have enticing news: think outside the cup! Your tea does not have to be consumed on its own. I'm not talking about having company to share the tea. Tea is great to pair with food, and you do not have to just limit it to cheese and chocolate, although that can be quite tasty, or to pairing tea with desserts. There is a vast world of entrees that can be a great match for your tea. In fact, when you have paired something well with the tea, you will notice that they enhance one another and it may change up your entire tasting.

Tea & Food Pairing Menu:

Appetizer

Food – Toasted pita served with a goat cheese spread drizzled with wildflower honey.

Tea – Assam (black tea) has malty notes that compliment the tart of the cheese and the sweet bites of honey.

Entrée

Food – Roasted green vegetable soup topped with croutons and a side of grilled poultry.

Tea – Dragonwell (green tea) has a subtle vegetative and nutty flavor that pairs nicely with the vegetable soup and mild chicken.

Dessert

Food - Warm crepe filled with a creamy vanilla ice cream topped with your favorite fruit, freshly picked and cut.

Tea – Tie Guan Yin (oolong tea), also known as Iron Goddess, adds to the creaminess of the dessert with its slightly sweet notes and fragrant aroma.

Practice pairing your tea and food lightly, and have fun during the development. That is truly the best way to discover what taste may fit your individual palate. If I have made you drooled anytime during this blurb, then next time you are preparing for a tea time, don't forget to set out that additional dish to accompany each sip.

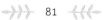

The Deeper Feelings Your Tea Emits

Sometimes we just need a quick minute. We need to be able to catch our breath, explore our thoughts and feelings, or even just pay closer attention to our surroundings. You know those times when you just feel like there are not enough hours in a day, or you wish there were two of you to get things accomplished? We need that minute to refresh, to embrace our existence, and to remind ourselves that life is great. We need to savor that minute when we get the chance. Tea can be that time for us.

Tea can be a connector that puts your life back together when you feel like it is slowly falling apart. It can be there for you to get your thoughts in order, settle down your mind, and grab hold of everything that feels like it is spiraling right before your eyes. How you use your time between steeps, sips and breaths is entirely up to you and you only.

Yet, tea can also be disconnecting. While tea is something that can get you to really think during your teatime, perhaps what is more revitalizing is what we are *not* thinking about. Aside from any company, when drinking tea, there is really only you and the tea. All else is pushed to the side. What do you sincerely need to worry about when everything is absent? Tea can take you away from the negative and push the positive forward. Instead of all the thoughts you have, you can focus on just your feelings. Empty your mind and let all those bad judgments and worries get erased.

It's Whom You Share It With

Before you began to steep your tea, did you set out tea ware for one or more people? Embrace being in the present and allow yourself to enjoy and notice those you share your cup with. After all, one of the most enjoyable characteristics of tea is the fact that it brings people, young or old, friends or strangers, all together. Pouring tea for yourself and others is the most satisfying kind of ritual. It allows you to connect with the company gathered for your tea service and to unwind together. Even in a world of differences, there is something we can all share in similarities: Tea.

When I first started to enjoy tea, it was not for the beverage. Sure, as a child I thought my sugary and creamy strawberry-flavored tea was delicious, and I definitely loved it. However, I was fonder of the idea behind it and the extraordinary time it created between my mother and sister. I knew our teatime was the one time we could get together, relax and just focus on our sips and talks. It was the perfect excuse for bonding time, and all conversations had around our cups of tea drew us in for what felt like hours.

However, indulging in tea alone is another special thing that should not be taken for granted. Sometimes you need to be alone to enjoy your time being yourself, and what better way to do that than with tea by your side? You can always think of others around the world who are indulging in a cup of tea with you in this very moment. You may be alone physically, but there are several who are facing something similar with their tea and you afar. With tea we are all linked, no matter where we are and how we are enjoying the leaf. There is a good chance that while you are absorbing these words, I am savoring a taste from my teacup with you.

PART IV

Ending with an Empty Cup (The Final Sip)

It all comes back around to where you started – with that empty cup that you originally picked out. Now that you can see the bottom of the cup, what does it reveal? You were just given the chance to relax, take a breather and live in the moment all because of this enchanting leaf that turned into a delightful beverage. Reflect on what was just presented to you in all aspects. Think back to each step to get you where you are right now. Think back to each sip that was had. How did they make you feel?

INVIGORATED RELAXED INSPIRED

MOTIVATED POWERFUL

CALM RENEWED ENERGIZED COMFORTED

FULFILLED FOCUSED CHEERFUL

Keep a journal of your own for the thoughts and feelings the tea releases throughout the tasting, especially your final one. How you conclude can determine your ultimate opinions. However, at the end of the moment, the tea is not the only thing that matters. Preparing the tea properly is not the only thing that matters. Drinking the tea at the perfect temperature is not the only thing that matters.

What matters the most is that you are able to enjoy, appreciate and connect. These three things apply back to the tea, but also to you. Enjoy the taste of the tea, but also enjoy your own company. Appreciate the energy and hard work that went into the tea, but additionally appreciate the life you are making for yourself. Connect with the story behind the tea, but connect with your life purpose and authentic self.

Go into your tea session to feel. Feel any and all kinds of emotions: happiness, sadness, anger, fear. Focus on being able to experience all around you at that moment, instead of the steeped product only. Give yourself to the tea and let it help you become more aware to grow.

More Than A Cup

The fun and beautiful experience does not have to end with that final sip. This might be the part of the tea session where you begin to clean up by discarding your tealeaves. Try to ignore the trash here. Give the tea a new life, a new meaning, and a new opportunity to flourish. Stretch out the life of your tea even longer by re-steeping the same leaves and having another comparable experience, or take your spent tea leaves, place them in a jar with cool water in the refrigerator overnight for a cold steep in

the morning. Try adding the spent tea leaves into your favorite meals, sauces, dressing and desserts. Compost them to help produce a fresh, nutrient rich soil for your garden. Keep that one cup of tea going for as long as you can! It is worth more than a single steeping and satisfaction.

Caring for Your Tea Ware

The vessels for your tea—teapots, cups, strainers, infusers and more—can affect the beverage's full potential. The different shapes and designs can also make a great difference in how your tea ultimately tastes. But perhaps one of the most picturesque things your tea wares can do for the tea is show it off. Depending on the specific type of vessel used and how it was made, it can allow you to best judge and appreciate the movements of the tea as it expands to release its flavors and the true color of the liquor.

Various materials can be used to make tea wares.

Porcelain. Cast iron. Glass. Clay. Ceramic.

Each type of material has its own care requirements. Earlier, we touched upon the time and effort that most likely went into creating the tea ware that is a part of your teatime. Knowing that, in respect for the passion and hard work, properly caring for your tea ware is a great way to give thanks. It will also allow for them to last as long as possible and give you the opportunity to continue to share many more tea memories with them.

Wipe down your tea wares by hand when you are done with them. Use soft cloths – never scrub with abrasive fabrics. Use gentle cleaning supplies – never wash with harsh soaps.

The tea wares in front of you played a major role in your teatime. It is only right to show them the respect that they deserve.

The Storage for Your Tea

You have your personal space to enjoy your tea, but what about the space for your tea afterwards? Having a specific spot just for your tea and tea ware not only keeps everything together, but also creates a safe and secure place for them. Think of your tea ware as treasure that needs some place safe for keeping and safe for longevity. When we get a new diamond-studded jewelry or a new designer wristwatch, we don't just toss them somewhere quickly when we are done with them. We usually have a special spot for them on the dresser, in the box they came from, or in a safe. We do this for a reason. Whether you purchased them yourself or they were a gift, these items have a lot of value and you know without the proper care and space for them, they can be damaged or even get lost, just like your tea ware. They are priceless.

Store your tea ware on a shelf. Store your tea ware in a cabinet. Store your tea in a chest. Wherever you do, make it a sacred place for just tea-related pieces. Just make sure that after each use, your tea items are back in their spots. This way, whenever you are ready for tea again, you know where they will be and you can trust they are clean and prepared for those leaves to dance, whichever way you make that happen.

Conclusion

(This Is Just The Beginning)

You have reached the completion of your tea experience. Hopefully, it was gratifying during every big and small tea moment you and your tea shared. While you are technically finished, there is no real ending here. The tea can leave you inspired to make a second cup. What tea means to you is more important than what anyone else thinks because the spirit of tea is unique to us all. It needs to mean something. If it does not mean anything to that individual, then the spirit of tea can be lost.

Keeping up with welcoming all aspects of tea, big and small, can be a slightly daunting. It can seem too spiritual for some. It can seem like an excessive amount of work, and it can seem like it takes away too much time from your busy schedule. But guess what? You do not have to experience everything all at once, or even each time you want a cup of tea. Do it slowly, and over time, if that makes you more comfortable, or even just once to understand more of what these words convey. It is something I believe tea drinkers should at least practice on one occasion and continue if they feel guided to. Even though the destination is here, the journey through the tea leaves is what it is all about.

During my own tea journey, in order for me to really connect and participate with the leaf, I have to ignore tea snobbery and unplug from anything that would cause related distractions. I have to ignore the labels. I have to ignore the reviews. I have to ignore anything that would deter my reflections and actions. Despite what you may have just read, I actually do not consider myself to be quite spiritual. What I do believe is that what we put out into the universe can come to fruition with our mind's power. With each thing that brings tea to life, it is commonly said that tea contains the entire universe.

"Looking deeply into your tea, you see that you are drinking fragrant plants that are the gift of Mother Earth. You see the labor of the tea pickers; you see the luscious tea fields and plantations in Sri Lanka, China, and Vietnam. You know that you are drinking a cloud; you are drinking the rain. The tea contains the whole universe."

- Thich Nhat Hanh, How to Eat

The major part of moments with tea is still the tea itself. Focusing on the tea as opposed to our surroundings is one of the best ways to appreciate and savor, be grateful and inspired by the beverage. All extra elements are just to emphasize the pleasures the tea holds. Hopefully, you may now confidently see that your cup holds more "tea-spiration" than what may just be written on a tea tag or box.

Please stop worrying about doing tea "wrong" and follow your own tea path to find what works best for your happiness. If you find yourself not clear on how to know when you are properly enjoying your tea – you will feel it, trust yourself.

happy steeping & sipping,
LU ANN PANNUNZIO

P.S. If you want to share your own big or small moments you have had with tea, you can write to me at theteacupoflife.com or tag me on social media with #teaspiration.

ACKNOWLEDGEMENTS

My biggest thanks go directly to everyone behind the tea scenes. While I may not know many tea farmers and workers personally, I can feel your stories throughout the steeps of the leaves you have cultivated and processed for me. I know that my passion and love for tea would not be possible without each and every one of you and without tea I would not be where I am right now, sitting at my desk canvased in tea posters and quotes with a cup of tea writing this book and soon after my tea blog.

Thank you to my Mom and Dad for always supporting me and trying your best to understand my tea obsession. It's always fun when you occasionally join in!

Thank you to Luciana, as the dedication states, this book would not have existed without you.

I love you more (and it's possible!).

Thank you to Lucio for always having my best interests in mind and for all the times you had me make you a cup of tea. Those years of experience have certainly come in handy!

Thank you to Victor for taking time away from your Canadian tea plants for a few moments to be a part of this book journey with me.

Thank you to James for putting up with my endless tea ramblings and book thoughts. Thank you for pushing me to write, preparing me tea when needed and reminding me that my words will be heard.

Thank you to Hugo and the rest of the team at Mango for helping me bring my words to life. I could not have asked for a better publishing experience.

Lastly, thank you to all of my readers at www.theteacupoflife.com. I started The Cup of Life tea blog back in June 2011 with no idea of what it would become today. I never thought I would experience and learn so much about the tea world and I never thought I would meet so many incredible tea lovers. Through everything I have been able to experience there is still nothing more rewarding than being a part of such a wonderful tea community. I raise my teacup to you all.

24 Hours
of Inspiration

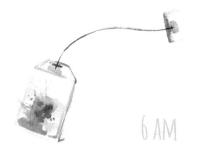

6 AM

"ALL OUR DREAMS CAN COME TRUE IF WE HAVE THE COURAGE TO PURSUE THEM."

- Walt Disney

"I THINK SELF-AWARENESS
IS PROBABLY THE MOST
IMPORTANT THING TOWARDS
BEING A CHAMPION."

– Billie Jean King

8 AM

"I FIND HOPE IN THE
DARKEST OF DAYS, AND
FOCUS IN THE BRIGHTEST."

– Dalai Lama

9 AM

"IT IS BETTER TO FAIL IN ORIGINALITY THAN TO SUCCEED IN IMITATION."

– Herman Melville

"ALWAYS BEAR IN
MIND THAT YOUR OWN
RESOLUTION TO SUCCEED IS
MORE IMPORTANT THAN
ANY ONE THING."

—Abraham Lincoln

11 AM

"STRIVE NOT TO BE OF SUCCESS, BUT RATHER TO BE OF VALUE."

— Albert Einstein

NOON

"FAILURE IS THE CONDIMENT THAT GIVES SUCCESS ITS FLAVOR."

– Truman Capote

"MASTERING OTHERS IS STRENGTH. MASTERING YOURSELF IS TRUE POWER."

— Laozi

2 PM

"WHY FIT IN WHEN YOU WERE BORN TO STAND OUT?"

— Dr. Seuss

"NOT ALL OF US CAN DO
GREAT THINGS, BUT WE CAN
DO SMALL THINGS WITH
GREAT LOVE."

– Mother Teresa

4 PM

"INNOVATION
DISTINGUISHES BETWEEN A
LEADER AND A FOLLOWER."

— Steve Jobs

5PM

"Tread softly;
Breathe peacefully;
Laugh hysterically."

– Nelson Mandela

6 PM

"If you're going through hell, keep going."

– Winston Churchill

"WHAT SEEMS TO US AS BITTER TRIALS ARE OFTEN BLESSINGS IN DISGUISE."

— Oscar Wilde

8 PM

"To be yourself in a world that is constantly trying to make you something else is the greatest accomplishment."

— Ralph Waldo Emerson

9 PM

"Things work out best for
those who make the best
of how things work out."

— John Wooden

10 PM

"THERE IS SOME GOOD IN
THIS WORLD, AND IT'S
WORTH FIGHTING FOR."

— J.R.R. Tolkien

"Success is liking yourself, liking what you do, and liking how you do it."

— Maya Angelou

MIDNIGHT

"Only put off until tomorrow what you are willing to die having left undone."

– Picasso

I AM

"NOTHING CAN BE DONE WITHOUT HOPE AND CONFIDENCE."

– Helen Keller

2 AM

"As we look ahead into the next century, leaders will be those who empower others."

– Bill Gates

"IF YOU'RE WALKING DOWN
THE RIGHT PATH AND YOU'RE
WILLING TO KEEP WALKING,
EVENTUALLY YOU'LL
MAKE PROGRESS."

— Barack Obama

4 AM

"Fortune sides with him who dares."

— Virgil

5 AM

"HOPE IS A GOOD BREAKFAST, BUT IT IS A BAD SUPPER."

— Francis Bacon

Lu Ann Pannunzio is a tea enthusiast and writer based in Ontario, Canada. When not drinking tea, Lu Ann finds other ways to incorporate the beverage into her life. She shares her steeps, tea infused recipes and crafts on her blog, **The Cup of Life** and across social media.

theteacupoflife.com | Facebook.com/theteacupoflife

Twitter: @theteacupoflife | Instagram: @teaaholic

CPSIA information can be obtained
at www.ICGtesting.com
Printed in the USA
BVOW05s2153071116
466898BV00006BA/8/P